Thorburn's Naturalist's Sketchbook

With an Introduction by

Robert Dougall

Book Club Associates
London

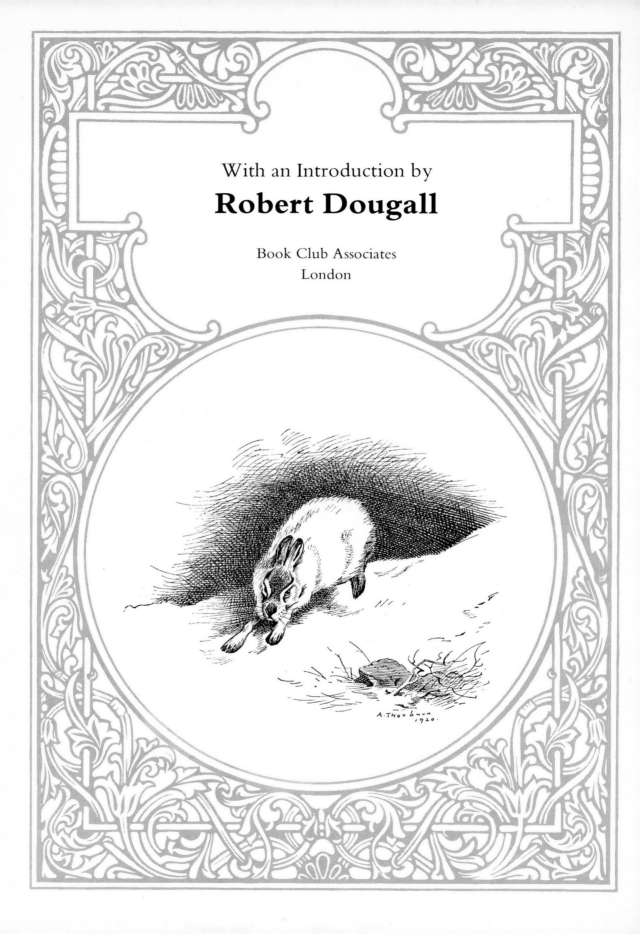

Thorburn's Naturalist's Sketchbook

This edition published 1977 by
Book Club Associates
By arrangement with
Michael Joseph Limited

Illustrations and text by Archibald Thorburn,
first published 1919 in *A Naturalist's Sketch Book*
This edition © Rainbird Reference Books Limited 1977,
and reproduced by permission of The Tryon Gallery.

The line drawings listed below are reproduced from
Thorburn's *British Mammals*, London, 1920–1, as follows:
page 1 Stoat, from Volume 1, page 76
     2 Mountain Hare, from Volume 2, page 33
     3 Roe Deer, from Volume 2, page 49
     6 Black Rat, from Volume 2, page 14
     9 Badger, from Volume 1, title page
  134 Wild Cattle, from Volume 2, page 54

The quotation on page 6 is from the obituary of
Thorburn that appeared in the *Ibis,* January 1936, 13th series,
vol. VI: 205–7, and is reproduced by kind permission of
the British Ornithologists' Union.

This book was designed and produced by
Rainbird Reference Books Limited, London
House Editor: Perry Morley
Designers: Pauline Harrison and Chris Sorrell

Text filmset and printed by Jolly & Barber Ltd, Rugby
Bound by Dorstal Press Ltd, Harlow

Contents

Editorial Note

In this new edition, we have reproduced from the 1919 edition almost all of Thorburn's sketches and the text in its entirety except for a few references to illustrations which have not been included here. Since the illustrations have been slightly rearranged to suit the small format, we have amended the text where necessary to take account of their new positions. We have added eleven plates from *British Birds* and four from *British Mammals*, and a few engravings from the latter; notes identifying these appear in square brackets or on page 4.

A word of caution: we felt that it was more appropriate to accompany the illustrations by the artist's original notes than to attempt to update information about the species shown and we must emphasize that the text is not up-to-date. Recent information on the distribution of these species in the British Isles as well as more plates by Thorburn may be found in *Thorburn's Birds*, edited with an introduction and text by James Fisher, revised by John Parslow (London, 1976) and *Thorburn's Mammals*, with an introduction by David Attenborough and notes by Iain Bishop (London, 1974).

Introduction
by Robert Dougall

It seems to me a cause for no small rejoicing that Archibald Thorburn's *A Naturalist's Sketchbook*, now a rare collector's piece, is being revived in this edition for a new generation to enjoy. It first appeared when the artist was at the height of his powers in 1919. He was then aged 59 and living at Hascombe, near Godalming in Surrey, where he resided until his death on 9 October 1935.

A few months later his great friend and fellow artist, George Lodge, called him a great ornithological artist, who 'at once demonstrated . . . his infinite superiority to all contemporaries in the same line of work. . . . He had a wonderful gift for placing his bird subjects in harmonious surroundings. . . . Whether he was painting a large picture of a whole covey or flock of birds or merely a scientific depiction of a single bird for a book illustration, his method and execution were equally admirable. . . . He appeared to visualize a subject so well before beginning to paint it that his work was very rapid, and wonderfully fluent and direct.' Lodge then spoke of another of his characteristics that shines through everything he did: 'Thorburn was a man of most lovable qualities, very modest about his own work, but never reticent about his methods of producing it, and always ready to impart his knowledge to others in the most generous way.'

In a sense, his work bridged the differing techniques of the nineteenth and twentieth centuries and in both he was supreme. It is strange to think that much of his meticulous observation of birds and mammals may have come from a disciplined study of the anatomy of Greek statues. That was in his boyhood days of the 1860s and '70s in Scotland, when he was greatly influenced by his father, Robert Thorburn, R.S.A., A.R.A., who was portrait miniaturist to Queen Victoria.

Then, after his education at Dalkeith and in Edinburgh, he came to London to study at art school in St John's Wood. As a young man of 20 he first exhibited at the Royal Academy and the painting selected owed much to his Scottish background – 'On the Moor'.

In a few years he won recognition as a leading illustrator and soon attracted the attention of one of the foremost ornithologists of the day, Lord Lilford, who was working on a major treatise, *Coloured Figures of the Birds of the British Islands* (1885–98). The original artist chosen, J. G. Keulemans, fell ill, and Thorburn was commissioned to complete the work. He learned much and benefited greatly from his association with Lord Lilford, who was the most exacting of men.

While still engaged on this project, he met Constance Mudie, whom he married in 1896. They continued to live in London and he was by this time greatly in demand as an illustrator of scientific and sporting books. He was also an enthusiastic supporter of the then newly formed Royal Society for the Protection of Birds and in 1899 started a long tradition when he painted its first Christmas card. It was a study of roseate terns, with a verse by the Poet Laureate, Alfred Austin. In all Thorburn did 19 Christmas cards and the last was of a goldcrest: it was also the last thing he painted before his death, after a long and painful illness. The originals were all given to the Society and sold in aid of funds: prices ranged from 10 to 30 guineas.

There is no doubt that Thorburn's paintings did much to stimulate a growing interest in birds and their place in nature; in recognition of his services to bird protection he was elected a vice-president of the Society in 1927. *A Naturalist's Sketchbook* was one of five books he wrote and illustrated himself between 1915 and 1926. It is a special example of his art and Sir Hugh Gladstone, the Scottish historian and ornithologist, said of it: 'Some of these sketches – done, as they must have been, in but a few minutes – are, perhaps, the most intimate and fascinating examples of his skill.'

This new edition has 49 colour and over 90 monochrome illustrations, most of which are reproduced from the original book. Thorburn had gathered them from various sketchbooks and portfolios and they span about 30 years of his life. Some of the sketches were preliminary drawings for two of his other books, *British Birds* and *British Mammals*, and so a few colour plates from these works have also been included for interest and comparison.

I should like to stress that the text is the identical and rather generalized one Thorburn wrote over half a century ago. Thus, the essential character of his original publication has been faithfully retained. It is also interesting to note some of the changes that have taken place in the distribution of birds since his day – particularly the gains. Noteworthy among them is the osprey, whose disappearance 'banished and exterminated by the egg collector' the kindly genius so lamented. How delighted he would have been to know that since 1950, when one pair bred successfully at the now famous Loch Garten eyrie on Speyside, this splendid fishhawk has spread out elsewhere in the Highlands and the population has built up to 14 pairs. A happy thought too that over 1 500 acres of the ancient Caledonian pine forest and moorland, centred on Loch Garten, have now been acquired by the RSPB as a nature reserve for all time. Incidentally, it is heartening, too, to know that the Society has flourished exceedingly and now numbers a quarter of a million members.

In Thorburn's day the black and white wader, the avocet, the Society's emblem, was known only as 'a rare straggler'. It constitutes another conservation triumph that since these elegant birds tentatively returned to breed in Suffolk after World War II, successful colonies have now been established at Minsmere and on Havergate Island. Thorburn would also have rejoiced to know that the snowy owl has bred successfully in most years since 1967 on the tiny Shetland Isle of Fetlar to become Britain's rarest breeding bird.

Yet another enterprise which he would be sure to approve is the attempt being made by the Hon. Aylmer Tryon to re-establish the great bustard in its former haunts on Salisbury Plain. In his capacity as a leading wildlife art connoisseur and director of a famous London gallery, Aylmer Tryon is also one of those best qualified to give a final assessment of Thorburn's place in the world of natural history illustration. In his opinion: 'No other artist has achieved so well the softness of fur or feather, nor captured the wonderful colouring of the sheen of a drake mallard's head or of a cock pheasant in snow. His pencil sketches from life, too, so essential for success, have a delicacy of touch unsurpassed by others. Archibald Thorburn was, in my view, the best of all illustrators of British wildlife.'

These are words with which most people will heartily concur.

Author's Preface

The series of water colour and pencil sketches reproduced in this volume have been gathered from various sketch books and portfolios, representing part of the congenial though by no means easy labour of some thirty years, and were drawn mostly direct from life in many parts of the British Islands, while a few pictures, showing the birds in their natural surroundings, have been added.

Looking at things with the eye of the ordinary lover of nature, one can only attempt to represent with brush and pencil the wonderful beauty of the living creatures around us, though perhaps more of the true spirit and sense of movement may sometimes be suggested in sketches than in more elaborate and finished pictures. The chief essential is to acquire the faculty of observing and noting down the many subtle differences in pose and little tricks of habit in different species, and this knowledge can only be obtained by patient watching.

To quote the words of the late J. Wolf, the most original observer of wild animal life I have ever known, 'We see distinctly only what we know thoroughly.'

A short description of the different subjects has been added as an aid to the identification of the various species in the Plates.

Hascombe,
Godalming, *July* 1919

AT

Golden Eagle

This fine bird is still fairly plentiful in the wilder parts of the Scottish Highlands, where, owing to the protection afforded by the deer forests, it is not even rare as a breeding species.

The eyrie is usually placed on a ledge in some rocky cliff and occasionally in trees. A typical nest I had the opportunity of visiting on several occasions lately contained one white downy eaglet and consisted of a large mass of dead heather and sticks placed on the upper part of a sloping ledge covered with turf.

ferns, and woodrush, the latter plant being invariably used as a lining to the nest.

As I believe is usually the case, the nest had a northerly aspect to shield the eaglet from the heat of the mid-day sun and on looking upwards one could see it was well protected from the weather by overhanging rocks, while below the precipice fell sheer into the waters of a loch.

The sketch opposite represents the Golden Eagle in repose, with loosened plumage revealing the grey downy feathering on the flank of the bird, the sketch below the attitude when feeding, both sketched from life.

Golden Eagle

The figure above shows the Golden Eagle in flight about to clutch and carry off his prey, when he always uses his talons for the purpose.

In spite of his considerable weight, the bird rises with great ease and buoyancy, often soaring in wide circles and appearing to float in the air without effort. As shown in the sketch, the pinion feathers of the wing are separated during flight.

The sketch opposite gives the back view of a Golden Eagle when at rest.

Golden Eagle

The sketches of the Golden Eagle's talons taken direct from nature show how the claws interlock when the bird seizes his victim, making it next to impossible for any unfortunate hare or other quarry to effect its escape when once securely grasped.

The lower part of the tarsus and foot serve as an easy means of distinguishing this species at any time from the White-tailed or Sea Eagle, figured on page 16, the latter having the lower half of the tarsus unfeathered and the toes plated with large scales, whereas in

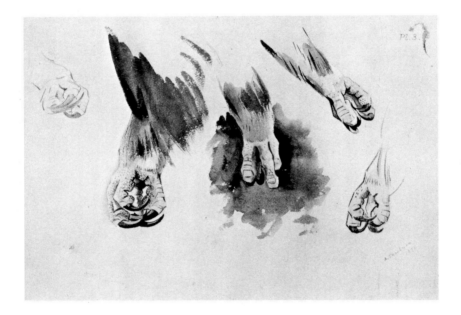

the Golden Eagle the legs are clothed with feathers as far as the base of the toes, which are covered with a network of small plates with three or four broad scales next the claws.

In adult plumage the two species may be easily known, the Sea Eagle having a white tail, while that of the other is dull grey, barred with a darker tone.

[The Golden Eagle shown opposite is reproduced from Plate 32 of Thorburn's *British Birds*, London, 1915–18.]

Pl. 32

White-Tailed or Sea Eagle

This bird may now be considered extinct as a breeding species in the British Islands, except possibly in the Outer Hebrides, though it was at one time apparently more numerous than the Golden Eagle.

Usually placing its eyrie in precipitous cliffs on the sea coast it was outlawed by the shepherd and crofter and finally extirpated by the ruthlessness of the egg collector.

Immature migratory individuals from the northern continent of Europe may still be looked for along our coasts during autumn and winter, being easily distinguished from the adults by their dark tails and generally darker brown plumage.

In character this species has more of the vulture than the Golden Eagle, but though partial to dead fish and carrion found on the shore, it also frequently destroyed lambs as well as rabbits on the sheep farms and warrens.

Common Buzzard and Osprey

The Buzzard is not uncommon in many parts of Scotland, in the Lake District of England as well as in Wales, while in Ireland it has disappeared except as a spring and autumn visitant.

Owing to the neglect of game preserving during the late war, it appears to have become more numerous in the last few years, and on account of its sluggish habits and fondness for rabbits, moles, fieldmice and other small rodents, it does little harm to winged game, and spends much of its time sitting on some stony hillside or soaring with a style of flight not unlike that of the Golden Eagle.

In Scotland the nest is generally placed in a steep cliff, though in wooded districts it is built in trees.

The two sketches above show the Buzzard in repose.

The figure above gives the attitude of the Osprey when feeding, sketched from life in the Zoological Gardens of London.

At one time to be found breeding on various Highland lochs, this bird has now been banished and exterminated by the egg collector. The ancient nesting places, usually a conical rock, ruined building, or weathered pine on an island, are still there, and although situated among most beautiful surroundings have lost much of their charm by the Osprey's disappearance.

The food, consisting entirely of fish, is obtained by a sudden plunge from above, the slippery prey being firmly held by the long curved claws and roughened toes which distinguish this species.

Iceland Falcon and Greenland Falcon

On the opposite page are shown sketches from life of the two typical northern Falcons, that on the left-hand side a native of northern Greenland, and the other a darker bird inhabiting Iceland as well as southern Greenland.

The ground-colour of the first-mentioned species is pure white at all stages, whereas in the Icelander it is grey or brown.

These birds, as well as a still darker species now known as the Gyr Falcon (the three in former days were apparently classed as one under this name), were much sought after in the days of falconry and were prized on account of their great docility and powerful flight.

The Greenlander in the Plate was an extremely tame and gentle bird and when sitting for her portrait would allow one to turn the block on which she rested without showing any fear or changing her position.

All these northern Falcons have a certain noble and distinguished bearing, too subtle to give expression to in a picture, and kill their prey in a truly sporting manner by a lightning stoop from above. They feed chiefly on ducks and ptarmigan.

Iceland Falcon and Greenland Falcon

The two pencil sketches reproduced on this page were taken from life in the Gardens of the Zoological Society of Scotland, Edinburgh.

The Iceland Falcon appears to visit the British Islands less frequently than its near relation the Greenland Falcon, which, living

in a more severe climate, is often compelled to wander southwards in winter.

[The female Greenland Gyrfalcon (left) and the male Iceland Gyrfalcon (right) shown opposite are reproduced from Plate 36 of Thorburn's *British Birds,* London, 1915–18.]

Pl. 36

A. Thorburn 1914

Greenland Falcon. ♀   Iceland Falcon. ♂   3.

23

Peregrine Falcon

The Peregrine, the best known of our British Falcons, is found breeding in suitable places from the Shetlands to the Scilly Islands and is also plentiful in Ireland.

The nest, consisting of a hollow scraped out on an earthy ledge of rock, is often tenanted by successive pairs of birds for many generations, and if one of the pair be destroyed its place is soon filled by another bird.

The female is considerably larger than the male as in other members of the family and in hawking language was always styled the 'Falcon,' the male, reckoned as about one-third less, being known as the 'Tercel' or 'Tiercel'. The Peregrine is a bird of high courage and intelligence, and is easily tamed for purposes of falconry, the best for training being the immature birds which are caught on passage, i.e. when they follow the flocks of migrating wildfowl which leave northern Europe in autumn for warmer climates.

The two sketches show the birds at rest after feeding, with loosened feathers and standing on one leg as is their usual habit.

Pl. 8

A.T.
Feb. 19. 1918.

Iceland Falcon and Peregrine Falcon

Opposite are studies of the Peregrine at rest, from watercolour sketches.

The right-hand sketch above gives the attitude of the Iceland Falcon in repose with ruffled plumage, taken on a stormy day in March. The left-hand study shows a back view of the Peregrine and gives roughly the proportionate size of the two species.

27

Merlin

The Merlin is the smallest of the resident British Falcons and is still not uncommon in moorland districts, where it nests on the ground among rocks and heather.

When trained it is chiefly used by falconers for flying at larks, while in a wild condition it feeds on pipits, larks, thrushes, and other small birds, though it will master a quarry as large as the Golden Plover. In the adult male the upper parts and wing coverts are mostly a beautiful slatey grey in colour, while in the female they are in general brown. The sketch above was taken from a young bird in its first plumage, showing the jesses and block used for trained hawks.

[The Merlin (bottom left) and other falcons shown opposite are reproduced from Plate 38 of Thorburn's *British Birds,* London, 1915–18.]

Hobby. ♂.
Merlin (♂. ♀. & young).
Kestrel. ♀
Red-footed Falcon. (♂. & ♀).
Lesser Kestrel. ♂.
Kestrel. ♂.

Goshawk and Hobby

The Goshawk sketched on a bow-perch at the bottom of the opposite page is an entirely different type of hawk from those described in the preceding pages, and in build and character may be considered a giant Sparrow Hawk. Fierce and rapacious and of great strength, it preys on hares, rabbits, squirrels, and other mammals, as well as on game birds and water fowl.

It is by nature a forest-loving species, and when trained is used chiefly for hares and rabbits.

The Goshawk is now rarely met with and never appears to have been common in a wild condition in the British Islands, though in former days it was resident and nested in the great pine forests of Rothiemurchus and Glenmore in Inverness-shire.

Accompanying the Goshawk are three studies from life of trained Hobbies.

The Hobby is a migratory Falcon annually visiting England, but rare in Scotland and Ireland. It likes a wooded district where large oaks are common and nests high up in the trees, usually occupying the former home of a crow or some other bird.

In form it is remarkable for the great length of its wings, which reach, when folded, beyond the tail.

Besides attacking small birds, it preys on dragon-flies, cock-chafers and other insects, while its great powers of flight enable it to master the Swallow, the Martin, and even the Swift.

It was formerly used in hawking, but is delicate in constitution and does not usually live long in confinement.

Kestrel and Hen Harrier

On the right of the opposite page is given a sketch of the Kestrel, the small Falcon, familiar to us under the name of Wind-hover, from its habit of hanging, while facing the wind, at some distance above the ground as if suspended by a thread, while searching for the mice and other rodents which constitute its food.

The Hen Harrier, represented on the left, is a sketch from life of the male bird in immature plumage. Now very rare, this species was once plentiful in the British Islands and acquired its name from the ravages it committed in the poultry yard. The flight is easy and buoyant, and when questing for food it quarters the ground in the most thorough manner, so that little escapes its notice. All the individuals of this species I have seen in captivity seemed of a dour and sullen disposition, and quite untameable.

Long.eared Owl.   Tawny Owl.
Barn.Owl   Short.eared Owl.

Tawny Owl

The two studies on this page show the Tawny Owl, also called the Brown or Wood Owl. On the mainland of Great Britain it appears to be more common than any of its family, though not known in Ireland except where artificially introduced.

In habits it is more nocturnal than any other British species, and its loud hooting notes may often be heard after dark.

The sketches show the bird with closed eyes as it usually appears during the daylight hours.

[The Tawny Owl (top right) and other owls shown opposite are reproduced from Plate 26 of Thorburn's *British Birds,* London, 1915–18.]

Barn Owl

The coloured sketches opposite were taken from a young Barn Owl before leaving the nest, which consisted of a mere collection of castings in a dove-cot in which a box had been placed for the purpose of inducing the birds to breed. The young remain in the nest until apparently fully grown and feathered, when there is little difference between them and their parents. The old birds were most regular in their habits, every evening at sundown regularly quartering their beats in search of mice and voles, as could be proved by an examination of the castings or pellets of fur and bones which the owl, like other birds of prey, disgorges.

Before leaving the young alone for the day, the parents would furnish a supply of mice which were placed beside the owlets. The feathers on the face of this species form a characteristic heart-shaped disk, as shown in the sketches.

Pl. 28

Eagle Owl. ♀.

Eagle Owl

The pencil sketch above of the Eagle Owl was drawn from life in the Zoological Gardens of London. Inhabiting the mountainous and wooded parts of the Continent of Europe, this fine bird only occasionally straggles to our shores. Owing to its size and great strength it can kill birds as large as the Capercaillie, as well as hares, rabbits and even fawns. Its cry is a loud sonorous 'Uhu'.

[The Eagle Owl shown opposite is reproduced from Plate 28 of Thorburn's *British Birds,* London, 1915–18.]

Snowy Owl

The Snowy Owl is an Arctic species and a winter visitor to the northern islands and mainland of Scotland, and occasionally to England.

A good deal of variation occurs in the plumage, some specimens being pure white with only a few dark dots and markings, while others, especially the females, are strongly marked with bars. Its food consists of the Lemming and Arctic Hare, beside Ptarmigan, Willow Grouse and other birds. The yellow eyes and rounded head of this owl give it a curious wild-cat expression.

38

A. Thorburn

at Lilford

Raven

Above is given a coloured study of the Raven, taken from life during the courting season in spring when the bird displays his glossy plumage at its best, and has a characteristic habit at this time of raising the crest as shown in the sketch.

The brain of the Raven is said to be more highly developed than that of any other bird, while his bold and masterful spirit has enabled him to hold his own in spite of every man's hand being against him.

Good care is taken by the birds in selecting a safe situation for the nest, which is constructed of sticks with a lining of wool or hair. One I have in my memory was placed on a steep cliff above the Atlantic, quite inaccessible from below, and only to be got at from above by the use of a rope.

Kingfisher

The water-colour sketch of the Kingfisher shown above was taken from a living specimen in the Zoological Gardens of London. This well-known bird is distributed over the greater part of the British Islands, though not so common as it might be were it not for the persecution it receives at the hands of bird-stuffers and others, and also by the owners of fisheries.

Seen perched on a dead bough or post on the lookout for minnows in the stream below, or darting like a meteor along its course, this little fisherman adds much to the charm of his surroundings.

Raven

On these two pages are given various life studies of the Raven showing the action of the bird feeding, or when, with open bill, he utters his loud harsh croak.

Hooded Crow, Raven and Jackdaw

The Hooded or Grey Crow is given in the top left sketch, and shows the attitude of the bird when uttering its cry.

A winter visitor to the eastern counties of England, this species is a common resident in the Highlands of Scotland. About Aberfeldy, on the Tay, and also in the area watered by the Clyde, where it meets its near relation, the Carrion Crow, the two species often interbreed.

Below left is given a study of the Raven showing the pose of the bird when suspicious, though keen to get in touch with some carrion.

The Jackdaw figured in the centre is a common and familiar British bird, inhabiting the country as well as the outskirts of towns.

It is easily distinguished from the other Crows by its small size, the ashen grey on the nape and sides of the neck, and pearly white eyes.

The sketch was taken from life by the aid of a field-glass in the neighbourhood of Edinburgh, where a colony of birds were nesting in the cavities of some old beech trees.

[The Magpie, Raven and Jackdaw shown opposite are reproduced from Plate 20 of Thorburn's *British Birds,* London, 1915–18.]

Pl. 26

Magpie.   Raven.   Jackdaw.

Needle-tailed Swift.

Swift.   Nightjar.   Alpine Swift.

Red-necked Nightjar.   Egyptian Nightjar.

Nightjar

Below are shown sketches of the Nightjar or Goatsucker, taken in Surrey by means of a field-glass. The bird, on being flushed, soon alighted on the branch of an oak, sitting, as they always do when at rest, with the body placed lengthways along the bough. It has been stated that the head is held level with or lower than the tail, but on this occasion it certainly was not so.

The female may easily be distinguished from the male as the bird takes wing, by the absence of the conspicuous white spots on the first three feathers of the wing and the two outermost tail feathers, which are peculiar to the male.

[The Nightjars and Swifts shown opposite are reproduced from Plate 23 of Thorburn's *British Birds*, London, 1915–18.]

Blue Titmouse, Coal Titmouse, Great Titmouse, Marsh Titmouse and Bearded Titmouse

These two pages show four species of British Titmice, all more or less common, and also the much rarer so-called 'Bearded Titmouse', which does not by rights belong to this family. Below, on the left, are given sketches of the Blue Titmouse. This is the familiar little blue-capped bird of our gardens and shrubberies.

On the right of the Blue Tit is the Coal Titmouse, always distinguishable by the white spot on the nape, as well as by the irregular broken line of the black cap where it meets the white on the cheeks and sides of the neck.

On the opposite page, at the top right, is shown a sketch of the Great Titmouse, or Ox Eye, easily known by his large size, by the black on the throat extending downwards to the tail, and also by his clear metallic notes in early spring which compose the song of his species.

Below him, the Marsh Titmouse is represented. This species is not at all uncommon in some parts of England, but local in its distribution. The crown of the head is deep black, and the colour in general more sober than in the other species depicted.

These sketches were all taken from wild birds attracted by a feeding table near a window.

The Bearded Titmice on the top left of the opposite page were taken from life in the Zoological Gardens of London, where they appeared quite happy and at home in a large out-door aviary. This species, though rare, is still to be found among the fens of Norfolk, and also in Devonshire.

It is a bird of the reed beds, nesting in the dense aquatic vegetation in summer and roving among the dead stems in winter, while supporting itself on the seeds of the plants which form its chief food supply.

The long black mustachial feathers on the cheeks have given the bird its name.

Brambling, Linnet, Redstart, Wren, Pied Wagtail and Yellow Hammer

In the lower right-hand corner of the opposite page are shown studies of the Brambling, and one of the Linnet.

The Brambling, a winter visitor to Great Britain, leaves us in spring for its breeding quarters in northern Europe. It is a handsome species, with finely-contrasted plumage of glossy black, white, and chestnut.

The Linnet may commonly be found about uncultivated land, where it nests among furze or other low bushes. The crimson forehead and breast of the adult male have given it also the name of Rose Linnet.

The upper right-hand sketch gives the Redstart, one of the most beautiful of our summer visitants. It is local in distribution, though not uncommon in favoured districts. The drawing was made from a bird haunting a roadside in Perthshire, where a pair were apparently nesting in an old stone wall.

In the upper left-hand side of the opposite page are two studies of the Wren. This bird does not always erect the tail, as usually shown in pictures of the species, but frequently lowers it as indicated in one of the sketches.

Immediately below the Wren, at the bottom on the left-hand side, are given sketches of the Pied Wagtail and Yellow Hammer, two of our familiar wild birds. The former is commonly to be seen in meadows and pastures, and in the breeding season is fond of the neighbourhood of buildings, where it often nests among climbing ivy or in recesses of stone walls.

The Yellow Hammer, or Yellow Bunting, is common everywhere, and hardly needs description. Its well-known song is continued till late in the summer, after the notes of most of the other songsters have ceased.

Hawfinch, Linnet, Redwing, Mistlethrush and Blackbird

Above, on the left are shown sketches of the Hawfinch and Linnet. The Hawfinch is locally distributed in Great Britain, and often overlooked owing to its shy and retiring habits, though its fondness for green peas and cherries frequently attracts it to our gardens if situated near its haunts. The kernels only of cherries, haws, and other fruits are eaten.

On the left of page 55 are some sketches of the Redwing, a regular winter migrant, which comes to our shores about the same time as the Fieldfare. Slightly smaller than the common

Song Thrush, to which it is closely related, it is easily distinguished by the rich chestnut colour of the flanks and under wing coverts, and also by the distinct yellowish eye-stripe.

Its summer home is in Norway, and other parts of northern Europe. Redwings are delicate creatures, and among the first to suffer hardship during prolonged frost and snow.

Next to the figures of the Hawfinch and Linnet, are given two sketches of the Mistle Thrush, also known as the Storm Cock from its custom of pouring forth its wild and desultory notes during the gales of early spring. Perched on a bough, and facing the wind and sleet, the bird from which the sketches were taken seemed quite at home, and rather to enjoy the blast than otherwise. This bird is our largest native British Thrush.

A sketch of the Blackbird is shown on the right, above.

Mistle-Thrush

Black-Throated Thrush
♂ & ♀.

Song-Thrush

Fieldfare

Redwing

Redwing

On this page are shown some sketches taken from a Redwing, previously described.

[The Thrushes shown opposite are reproduced from Plate 1 of Thorburn's *British Birds,* London, 1915–18.]

Fieldfare

On the opposite page is the Fieldfare, a winter visitor to the British Islands, usually arriving in October and leaving us in spring for its breeding quarters in northern Europe.

The slatey grey head and rump as shown in the sketch serve to distinguish it from our other thrushes. The Fieldfare breeds in colonies, the nests being often placed in birch trees near the ground.

It has never been known to nest in the British Islands, though often recorded as doing so by people who confuse this species with the Mistle Thrush.

Goldfinch and Greenfinch

On the right, above, and also on the opposite page are given various pencil studies from life of the Goldfinch, perhaps the most beautiful and interesting of all our British Finches. The soft delicacy of its tawny colouring, touched up with crimson, black, and gold, make a charming picture as the little bird perched on some downy thistlehead extracts the seeds which form its favourite food.

It is to be regretted that it is now not nearly so numerous as in former days though by no means scarce in some parts of the country.

On the left of page 60 are sketches of the Greenfinch, a common British species, which show the birds as they rest when sunning themselves on a tree top.

The yellow and green of the plumage and thick flesh-coloured bill serve to distinguish it.

Blackcock

The four coloured studies of Blackcock given here were sketched direct from nature by means of a field-glass by the side of the river Helmsdale, in Sutherland.

During the courting season in early spring, I have not found these birds difficult to approach if ordinary care be taken. Soon after dawn the old cocks meet at some chosen spot, often a grassy opening in a birch wood, where a kind of tournament is held, and various contests take place for the possession of the females.

On the following two pages may be seen some of the striking attitudes assumed by the Blackcock during this display as he proceeds along the ground with drooping wings and outspread lyre-shaped tail, producing at the same time a succession of whirring or crooning notes which, though soft in tone, may be heard at a considerable distance on a still morning.

Blackcock

These sketches of the Blackcock courting
were drawn from life near the Helmsdale,
Sutherland.

Pl. 26.

Red Grouse

Pl.28.

Red Grouse

Red Grouse

Here are various rough sketches from life of the Red Grouse in spring, taken from one of the birds in the Gardens of the Zoological Society of Scotland. Some of these show the attitude of the bird when uttering its well-known call. It may be noted that the comb over the eye in this species differs from that of the Blackcock in colour, being more of a scarlet than the other.

On this page are shown sketches in colour of a Red Grouse which lived for some time in the Gardens of the Zoological Society of Scotland in Edinburgh.

This bird soon became quite fearless and absurdly tame, and in the breeding season would challenge and attempt to attack anyone approaching its enclosure.

The picture on the page opposite represents a pair of this species among their natural surroundings of rock and heather.

The Red Grouse is peculiar to the British Islands, where it is abundant on hill and moorland, its nearest relation, the Willow Grouse, which turns white in winter, representing our bird in Scandinavia.

Ptarmigan

Coloured sketches of the Ptarmigan in autumn plumage are given on these two pages. The studies above were obtained by the help of a field-glass as the birds made their way down a stony slope high up among the haunts of these birds in one of the Scottish deer forests, during the month of October.

If once located, often a difficult matter to accomplish, unless the birds move or utter their grating call, they are easy to approach when the weather conditions are settled, and apart from the interest of their wild and picturesque surroundings, the birds have a certain charm

of their own which appeals to all lovers of nature. The landscape sketch on pages 126–7 shows the hill near where the birds were feeding, and indicates the rough and stony character of their territory.

The coloured picture opposite gives the plumage of the Ptarmigan a little later on in November, when the mottled grey of their feathers is beginning to change to the snowy white of winter.

Common Pheasant

The picture opposite represents Pheasants in winter.

There are practically no pure-bred birds left in our coverts to-day, the original dark-breasted Pheasant, showing no white on the neck, and introduced before the Norman Conquest, having mingled, first with the Ring-necked Pheasant from southern China, imported about the end of the eighteenth century, and later with various other races since introduced. A complete and excellent account of the various species may be found in Millais' *Natural History of British Game Birds*.

Mongolian Pheasant
and Common Pheasant

The figure above is the Mongolian Pheasant, one of the most beautiful of the family, and only introduced in recent years to our woods and coverts. It may easily be distinguished from the Common Pheasant by the broad white collar and whitish wing coverts.

On the right are given various studies of Pheasants taken from some birds in an aviary.

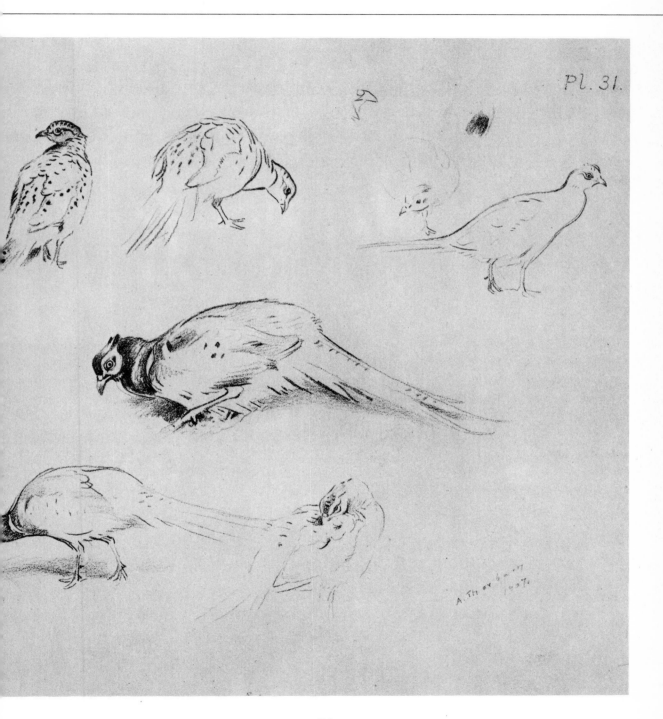

Pl. 31.

A. Thorburn
1917

Common Partridge
and Quail

The two figures on the left show the Quail, our smallest game bird and a summer visitant to the British Islands.

It is now much less plentiful than in former times, which may be attributed to the higher cultivation of land, and also no doubt to the netting of thousands of birds on migration in southern Europe. The sketch on the opposite page is from a water-colour study of a hen Partridge, and shows the difference in marking on the upper plumage which distinguishes the sexes.

Apart from the chestnut horseshoe on the breast of the male, which is either absent or only partly developed in the female, the latter has the scapular feathers and wing coverts barred with buff-coloured markings, whereas these are lacking in the male.

Common Partridge
and Common Pheasant

These two pages give some coloured studies from life of a cock Partridge basking, when with loosened feathers he shakes out the dust used for cleansing the plumage.

A female of this species I kept for some time in an aviary laid fertile eggs, which were afterwards hatched by a Bantam fowl. I believe this seldom happens when Partridges live in confinement, and are not allowed to select their own mates.

Some outline sketches of the Common Pheasant are also shown in the upper left-hand corner.

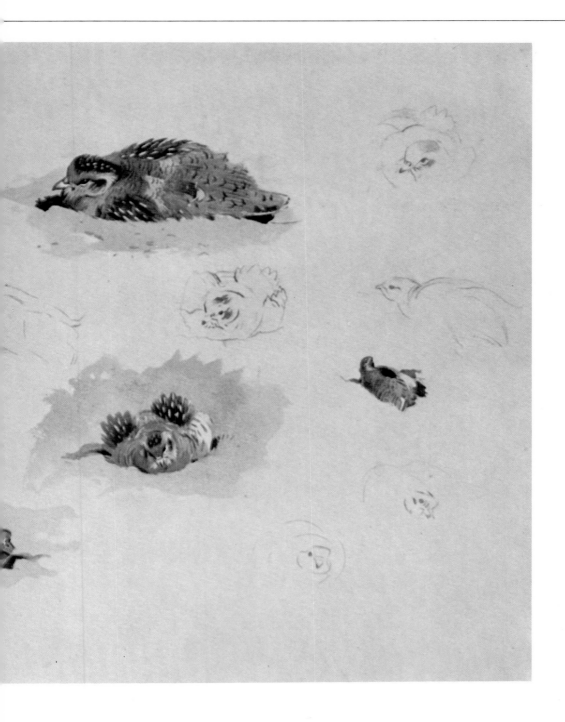

Common Partridge and Quail

Above is given a study from life of a Partridge, and opposite are four of the Quail.

Great Bustard

This splendid species, now extinct as a resident British bird, lingered in gradually diminishing numbers till 1838, when the last survivor was killed in Norfolk.

The coloured sketches shown were taken from a bird in confinement, and give some of the extraordinary attitudes assumed by the male during the period of courtship.

It is still found in some numbers in suitable places on the Continent of Europe, while attempts made to re-establish it in its old haunts in England have met with no success, for when once an indigenous species like the Great Bustard has been thoroughly exterminated, it is extremely difficult to restore it.

Cormorant, Shag and White Stork

Pl. 36.

The Cormorant, shown in the sketches on the left-hand side of both these pages, is a common bird along the rocky parts of our shores, and on the north-east coast of England and eastern side of Scotland appears to be more plentiful than its near relation the Shag, or Green Cormorant, though the latter species prevails in many parts of the west.

The sketches show the adult Cormorant in nuptial plumage, when the crest and white thread-like feathers on the head and neck are fully developed.

These decorations, as well as the white thigh patch, are lost later on in the summer.

A colony of breeding birds is always interesting, as they can then be more easily approached than on other occasions.

I have had the opportunity of visiting one of these colonies, on an island off the west coast of Sutherland in the month of May, which contained many nests placed on ledges at various levels on a steep sea cliff, some occupied by sitting birds, others guarded by their owners

standing by, as at this time no eggs are safe from the attacks of marauding Gulls or Hooded Crows.

The Shag, Green or Crested Cormorant, figured on the right of page 84, is a smaller, slimmer, and more elegantly-formed bird than the Common Cormorant, and in early spring assumes a curved tuft-shaped crest as shown in the sketches of this species.

The White Stork, shown above, right, is a scarce wanderer to our shores, though breeding regularly in many parts of Continental Europe.

It has never been known to breed in Great Britain in recent times, but Dr Eagle Clarke has drawn attention to an old record (*Scottish Naturalist,* 1919, p. 25) of this species having nested on the top of the Church of St Giles, Edinburgh, in the year 1416.

The white plumage of the Stork has usually a dingy soiled appearance; this, I am told, even occurs in wild specimens.

Gannet and Heron

On the left-hand side of this page are given two sketches of the Gannet, or Solan Goose.

This species breeds in colonies on various rocky islands in British waters, two of the best known being those on the Bass on the eastern, and Ailsa Craig on the western side of Scotland. There are also breeding stations on the St Kilda group of islands, Sulisgeir, Outer Hebrides, Suliskerry, west of the Orkneys, Grassholm, off the Welsh coast, the Skelligs and Bull Rock, Ireland, the latter station being the most southerly in Europe. The Gannet, formerly bred on Lundy Island, its only English breeding place, but is now extinct there.

The sketch of the Common Heron given on the right-hand side of this page shows the attitude of the bird when standing motionless by the edge of a pool, ready for any prey that may come within reach of its long and pointed bill. According to the late Lord Lilford, the Heron does not transfix fishes by the bill, but seizes them between the points of the mandibles.

[The Herons shown opposite are reproduced from Plate 40 of Thorburn's *British Birds,* London, 1915–18.]

Little Egret. Buff-backed Heron. Purple Heron.

Common Heron. Great White Heron.

Bittern

A study of the Bittern is given above. Before the draining of the fens and bogland became common in the British Islands, this bird was numerous in such parts of the country, where in the breeding season its deep booming notes were constantly heard at night.

At one time the Bittern ceased to exist as a breeding species in England, but thanks to the protection it has received, it is now re-established in some of its old haunts in Norfolk, where it appears to be yearly increasing in numbers, and its strange love-song may now again be heard in the marshes.

The sketch shows the curiously marked and spotted plumage, which serves to hide the bird among the dead reeds and sedges in which it seeks concealment by day.

[The Bitterns and other members of the Heron family shown opposite are reproduced from Plate 41 of Thorburn's *British Birds*, London, 1915–18.]

Pl. 41.

Glossy Ibis.
Common Bittern.

Night-Heron
Little Bittern.   Squacco Heron.
American Bittern.

Golden Plover, Grey Plover and Curlew

On these two pages are given various sketches from life of the Golden and Grey Plover, and also of the Curlew, distinguished by its long curved bill.

The Golden Plover is a resident, nesting on moorlands mostly in the northern parts of the British Islands and flocking to the low ground and mud-flats in winter, while the Grey Plover is best known as a bird of passage, never breeding in this country. Apart from the

larger size and silvery colour of the latter, the bird differs from the Golden Plover in possessing a small hind toe which is absent in the other, while under the wing the axillary feathers are black instead of white.

The Curlew is a well-known bird on many of the moorland districts in the British Islands in summer and moves down to the coast in winter.

Woodcock

The lower sketches on the opposite page give details of the Woodcock's plumage, also the bill and feet of the bird. On the wing feathers may be seen the intricate pattern of brown, black and buff, which imitate so closely the fronds of dead bracken and other foliage in the leafy coverts where the bird loves to conceal itself when resting, though often betrayed by its large dark eye.

Above is a sketch of the Woodcock in winter when this species suffers much during prolonged spells of frost and snow, as their food supply, consisting chiefly of worms, is then cut off.

A remarkable fact in the history of the Woodcock is the habit the bird has of carrying her young, which has long been known, but I think never so clearly described as in an account of this performance by Mr George Brooksbank in the *Scottish Naturalist* for 1919, pp. 95, 96, from which I have taken the following extract: 'On 14th June, 1918, I flushed a Woodcock from some bracken in an open space among the rhododendrons growing near the top of an exposed rocky hill. She began to fly straight away from me up wind, but on meeting the full force of the blast as she rose, she turned and came back close past me, and I was able to see that she was carrying a small young one. Her flight was laboured and unusual, and her tail was much depressed, so that her position in the air recalled that of a wasp when carrying a fly. The wind was strong and she quickly dipped over the rock or cliff a little way behind me. On going back and cautiously looking over the edge I saw her standing on a sort of ledge not far off and rather below me, but facing my way – up wind – and I could also see the young one crouched at her feet between her legs. As soon as she caught sight of me, she bent her neck and pushed the young one securely into position with her bill, raising her wings as she did so, and flew off out of sight down among the trees below. . .

'The young bird was carried close to the old one's body and well concealed by the lowered tail. In fact, from behind it would not have been possible to see it at all, and it was only when the old bird flew past me, or was facing towards me, that I could tell that a young one was being carried.'

Brent Goose and Bean Goose

PL.41.

A sketch of the Brent is given above. This small dark Goose is a winter visitor from the Arctic regions, and chiefly frequents the Shetlands, Orkneys, and eastern shores of Great Britain as well as the Irish coast. The birds often congregate in immense flocks, which are much sought after by punt gunners.

The Brent keeps to the sea and never comes inland unless by accident.

On page 95 the Bean Goose is figured. This species visits us in autumn from its breeding grounds in northern Europe, and may be distinguished from the Greylag and White-fronted Geese by the black nail at the point of the bill.

These three species, and also the Pink-footed Goose are known to shore shooters as 'Grey Geese', and are larger than the Brent and Bernacle, which are the so-called 'Black Geese'.

I have noticed that these two groups have each a characteristic method of feeding, the Grey Geese nibbling the grass in a slow deliberate manner, whereas the Brent and Bernacle snip the blades with a much quicker movement of the head and neck, more like the action of a common fowl when eating.

Pl 42.

96

White-Fronted Goose, Brent Goose, Sheld-Duck, Gadwall, Shoveler, Pintail, Tufted Duck and Scaup

In the lower left-hand corner in this Plate are sketches from life of the White-fronted Goose. This species is a winter visitor to the British Islands, more abundant on the western and southern coasts than on the eastern side of Great Britain, except in the neighbourhood of the Moray Firth, the Shetlands and Orkneys. It is easily recognised by the white frontal patch bordered by black, and the prominent black bars on the lower part of the breast.

Opposite the White-fronted Goose on the right-hand side of the Plate, is a sketch showing the head and shoulders of the Brent Goose, also figured on page 94. This shows the distinctive character of the head and neck in this small Goose, which also applies to the Bernacle, viz., the shortness of bill and absence of the strongly-marked ridges in the plumage of the neck. Along with the Bernacle are sketches of the Gadwall, Shoveler, and Pintail.

The Gadwall is dull in colouring compared with the other British fresh-water ducks, though the plumage is marked by beautiful pencillings of black and grey, and it may always be distinguished by the pure white wing spot or speculum.

In habits it is quiet and unobtrusive, and closely resembles the Mallard, though more partial to the seclusion of quiet fresh-water pools than the other. The Pintail, figured next the Gadwall in the act of preening its breast feathers, is easily known by its long-pointed tail feathers, which have given the bird its name.

This graceful species is a resident and also a regular winter visitor to Great Britain, being more common on the mud flats and shores than on inland waters. It has lately increased as a breeding species, and now nests on Loch Leven as well as in other parts of Scotland.

In the upper right-hand corner of this Plate are given sketches of the Scaup, Pintail, Brent Goose, Tufted Duck and Sheld-Duck.

In the upper-left hand corner are the Tufted Duck, Pintail, Scaup, and Shoveler. The Tufted Duck is resident as well as a winter visitor to the British Islands, and has much increased of later years as a breeding species. Like the Scaup, it obtains its food by diving, the other ducks shown on this Plate being all of the surface-feeding kind.

If one compares living specimens of these two species it will be noticed that the shape of the mass of flank feathers differs, those in the Tufted Duck usually forming a concave outline, while in the Scaup this is convex. This point is indicated in the sketches, which were taken from life in the Gardens of the Zoological Society of Scotland.

Bean Goose, Bernacle Goose, Common Sheld-Duck, Garganey, Pintail, Tufted Duck and Eider Duck

Above is a sketch of the Bean Goose feeding, showing the characteristic angle in the neck when the bird is nibbling the grass blades on which it chiefly subsists.

On the left-hand side of the opposite page in the centre of the sheet of studies, is given a sketch of the Bernacle Goose feeding and of the Tufted Duck swimming, and above one of the Pintail.

Below these are outline sketches of the Eider Duck.

In the right-hand set of studies is one of the Garganey at the top and three of Sheld-Ducks below, also the head of a Brambling. The Garganey is best known as a spring visitor to England, and is chiefly found in Norfolk, where it breeds during the summer months. In colour it is beautifully marked with various shades of brown and bluish-grey. During the breeding season the male utters a curious rattling note.

The Common Sheld-Duck is plentiful on many parts of the coast where there are stretches of sand and bents which suit its habits.

This is a very handsome species, with crimson bill and strongly contrasting plumage of black, white, and rich chestnut.

It nests in burrows, sometimes using the disused home of a rabbit, at others excavating a tunnel for itself.

The lower sketch of the female Sheld-Duck shows a characteristic pose of the bird in spring.

Wigeon, Scaup and Eider Duck

The sketch on this page shows a male Wigeon when asleep, with bill tucked into the scapular feathers. The Wigeon is best known as a winter visitor to the British Islands, though some birds nest in the wilder parts of Scotland, and a few have been recorded breeding in the north of England and in Wales.

Included in the same sketch is a study of the Eider Duck at rest on shore, and the same bird is given opposite on the water.

When the females, whose nests provide the well-known eider-down of commerce, are sitting, the males may be seen at sea in the neighbourhood, when their curious crooning notes, which carry such a long distance across the water, may frequently be heard.

They are clumsy, ungainly birds on land, though graceful enough and quite at home in the water, and are splendid divers, going down to a great depth, even thirty feet or more, after the mussels on which they feed.

They breed as far south as the Farne Islands in England, along the east coast of Scotland, and are also very plentiful on the islands off the west coast of Sutherland, where I have had many opportunities of watching them.

The Scaup, shown in the middle portion of the sketch below, is another handsome diving duck, the drakes, with their dark glossy green heads and mantle of grey, and the ducks, easily distinguished by their brown plumage and large patch of white next the bill.

Like the Eider, they go down deep for the food, and may be seen in large numbers off the mussel-beds during winter.

Mallard, Teal and Pintail

Two studies of the Teal from life are given above, on the left.

This is a common British species, and nests regularly in many parts of our islands.

Next to the Teal, on the right, is a sketch of the Pintail, and opposite are others of the Mallard, or Wild Duck, the origin of our domestic Duck, and the most common and best known of this family.

A.T. Jan 7 - 1901

103

Gadwall, Shoveler, Teal, Garganey, Wigeon, Scaup, Tufted Duck and Eider Duck

On the right-hand side of this page are sketches of the Wigeon (female) and Shoveler (male and female), the latter species being easily known by the large spoon-shaped bill, and also by the deep chestnut on the lower part of breast, and

the glossy green head which mark the male bird.

The Shoveler has greatly increased in numbers in Great Britain during the last forty years, and frequents fresh water lakes in preference to the sea.

On the left-hand side of page 104 will be found sketches of the Wigeon, the American Wigeon, Shoveler, and Teal.

Below are two sketches of the Garganey feeding, showing the action of the

birds when paddling after insects in muddy water.

Above are sketches of Scaup, Tufted Duck, Pintail, Gadwall, and Eider Duck.

Great Black-Backed Gull, Turnstone, Ringed Plover and Smew

Pl. 47.

The sketch of the Great Black-backed Gull on this page, was taken by the help of a field-glass on one of the Scilly Islands where this fine bird is plentiful.

It may always be readily distinguished from the Lesser Black-backed Gull by its much larger size, darker mantle, and flesh-coloured legs, the latter species having the legs of a bright yellow tint.

The Great Black-backed is the largest resident British Gull, and usually selects for its breeding place an isolated rocky 'stack', where the two or three olive-brown, darkly blotched eggs are laid in a nest placed in some hollow among the turf or earth.

Below the Gull on the right is a study of the Turnstone, and on the left one of the Ringed Plover, both sketched on the Scilly Islands.

The studies of the Smew (male and female) shown opposite were taken from living specimens in the Gardens of the Zoological Society of London.

This beautiful little diving duck only visits us in winter, when it is not uncommon on the eastern coasts of Great Britain, though the full plumaged males, like the one figured in the Plate, are not often met with.

The peculiar shape of the black bars on the breast and flanks can only be seen to advantage in the living bird.

The food, consisting chiefly of small fishes, is obtained by diving, the prey when captured being securely held by means of the saw-like teeth with which the bill is furnished.

Tern

The slight sketches of Terns on this page were made on the shores of the Moray Firth in August, by means of a field-glass.

At this time of the year, when the young have left the nest, large flocks frequent the shore before starting on their southward journey to spend the winter in warmer seas. The most numerous are the Common and Arctic Terns, but the two species are not easily distinguished except when handled, the last mentioned having the bill of a uniform deep red, without the dark tip of the other bird's, the tarsus is shorter, the wings extend farther beyond the tail, while the under parts of the body are greyer in colour than in the Common Tern.

Whether flying, basking on the beach, or poising their slender bodies with uplifted wings on the top of a stake, they are the most graceful of birds and can be recognised from any gull when on the wing by a curious bounding action in their flight. [The Terns shown opposite are reproduced from Plate 71 of Thorburn's *British Birds,* London, 1915–18.]

Pl. 71.

Roseate Tern.

Sandwich Tern.
(Adults & young.)

Arctic Tern.
Common Tern.
Little Tern.

Wild Cat

On the left are given some sketches from life of the Wild Cat, a dour and untameable beast, yet full of interest to the naturalist. It is now very scarce and confined to the wilder parts of the Scottish Highlands, where the deer forests have served to protect it.

It may be distinguished from the domestic cat – whose offspring after running wild for a generation or two in the woods often assume the brindled colouring of the genuine wild animal – by its greater robustness of body, the thick and unpointed bushy tail and black soles of the feet.

The principal sketch was used for the picture of the Wild Cat in Millais' *Mammals of Great Britain and Ireland*.

[The line drawing shown below is reproduced from Volume 1, page 46, of Thorburn's *British Mammals,* London, 1920–1.]

Weasel

These sketches from life were made from a Weasel which, tempted by a vole already in the trap, found itself caught after eating its victim. After a great display of anger by this unexpected intruder it was safely transferred to more roomy quarters, and was later given its liberty.

Lithe and slim in body, and an expert in killing its prey, this little animal is most useful in ridding a garden of mice and voles, and will also hunt in the tunnels of the mole. Once to my surprise I found one caught in a mole trap after having wormed its head, shoulders and forelegs through the small iron ring, less than an inch in diameter, which acts as a trigger when the trap is set.

Woodmouse

On the right are some sketches from life of the Common Woodmouse. There are several varieties of this beautiful creature in the British Islands, the most handsome of all being the large Yellow-necked Woodmouse, which measures from nose to end of tail about $8\frac{3}{4}$ inches. Another large variety is that found in the Island of St Kilda.

Woodmice are easily tamed, and pretty creatures to watch in confinement, always keeping their fur in spotless condition, and spending a good part of their time in cleansing it. Even the tail is carefully licked over while held in position by the fore feet, as shown in the central sketch.
[The line drawing shown below is reproduced from Volume 2, page 7, of Thorburn's *British Mammals*, London, 1920–1.]

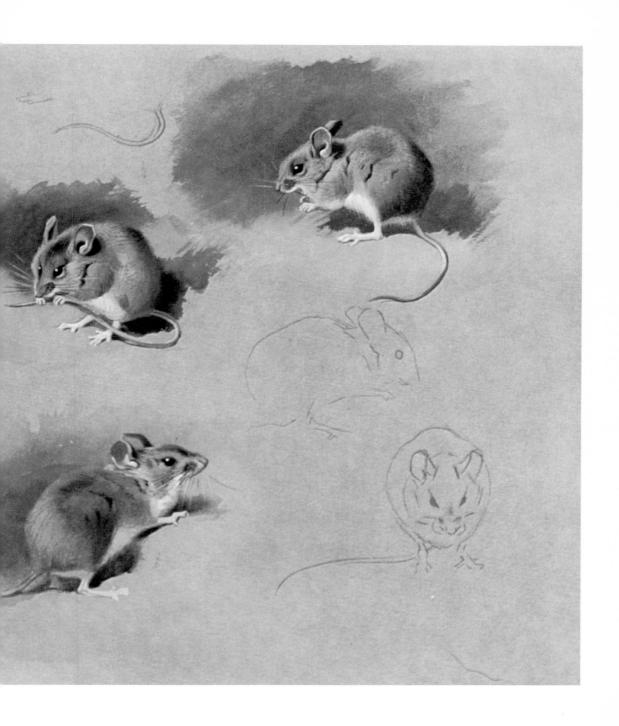

Fox

The studies of the Fox shown below and of the Otter on page 119 were taken from animals in the Gardens of the Zoological Society of Scotland, Edinburgh, and were made for a book on British mammals.

The Fox, though nocturnal in its habits, may often be seen abroad in daylight, but this seldom happens with the Otter. I have only once had an opportunity of watching the latter at close quarters in a wild condition, as it made its way along the banks and among the stones of a stream in Sutherland.

[The Fox shown opposite is reproduced from Plate 11 of Thorburn's *British Mammals,* London, 1920–1.]

Fox. $\frac{1}{3}$

Otter

[The sketch of the Otter shown above was made in the Gardens of the Zoological Society of Scotland, Edinburgh (see page 116).] [The Otter shown on the opposite page is reproduced from Plate 17 of Thorburn's *British Mammals*, London, 1920–1.]

Red Deer

Above are shown studies from life of Red Deer.

[The Red Deer shown on the opposite page are reproduced from Plate 37 of Thorburn's *British Mammals,* London, 1920–1.]

Pl 37.

Red Deer.

Wild Cattle

Pl. 53.

Above are shown studies from life of Wild Cattle.

The origin of the so-called Wild Cattle, now only to be found in a few enclosed parks in Great Britain, is uncertain, though there can be no doubt of their great antiquity. They are probably descended from domesticated animals which had taken to a wild life in the forests before historic times, and were later rounded up and enclosed in parks for their preservation. Few of these herds are now in existence, the best known being the Chillingham, Cadzow and Chartley breeds.

[The Wild Cattle shown on the opposite page are reproduced from Plate 40 of Thorburn's *British Mammals,* London, 1920–1.]

Wild Cattle. Cadzow.

Highland Pony

This sketch of the old breed of Highland Pony or Garron, was made many years ago in a Sutherland deer forest. On the animal are shown the deer saddle and breeching required for bringing home the stags, no easy task on a rough and steep hill-side.

Ptarmigan Hill, Sutherland

PL.55.

This landscape sketch gives a view of the 'Red Corrie', Glasven, and shows a typical bit of ptarmigan ground.

The birds make a home for themselves on these barren hills, where they shelter among the lichen–covered stones and rock, so closely resembling their plumage in colour.

On the lower slopes grows the beautiful Alpine plant, the Cushion Pink, *Silene acaulis*, decked with its rose-coloured flowers in early summer.

Eagle's
Hunting Ground

The sketch given here was taken high up on a Highland deer forest, and shows the hunting ground of the Golden Eagle, where he takes his toll of the Grouse and Ptarmigan.

Pl.57.

Snow-Covered Furze and Pines

These two sketches, taken after a heavy snowfall, were made as a background for Pheasants in winter.

Germander Speedwell, Dandelion and Plantain

This Plate shows sketches in colour of three of our common wayside plants, the Germander Speedwell on the left, the Dandelion in the centre, and the Plantain on the right-hand side.

Index

References in bold type are to illustrations. Other references are to the text.